GARY PLAYER'S GOLF CLINIC

DBI Books, Inc., Northfield, Ill.

- *Instruction by* **Gary Player**
- *Script by* **Iain Reid**
- *Drawings by* **Gary Keane**
- *From photographs by* **Sydney Harris**
- *Cover photography by* **Tony Roberts/Sportshot**
- *Publisher:* **Sheldon L. Factor**

Published by DBI Books, Inc., One Northfield Plaza, Northfield, Ill. 60093, a subsidiary of Technical Publishing, a company of the Dun & Bradstreet Corporation.

Arms and Armour Press, London G.B., exclusive distributors in South Africa and Zimbabwe.

ISBN 0-910676-23-2   Library of Congress Catalog Card #81-65104

TABLE OF CONTENTS

SECTION ONE—Swing Fundamentals

section one
Swing Fundamentals

Make a good start

THE *FIRST* DRIVE OF THE DAY IS VERY IMPORTANT, IAIN. IT CAN SET THE PATTERN FOR THE REST OF THE ROUND

SO I CONCENTRATE ON *TRANSFERRING MY WEIGHT* ONTO MY *LEFT* SIDE, AND FINISHING WITH MY *HANDS HIGH*

SIMILARLY, IF MY *FIRST PUTT* IS A GOOD ONE, IT GIVES MY *CONFIDENCE* A TREMENDOUS BOOST

I, THEREFORE, TRY VERY HARD TO KEEP MY HEAD *ABSOLUTELY STILL*, AND TO HAVE A *FULL FOLLOW-THROUGH*

IN GOLF, A *GOOD START* IS INVALUABLE!

The key to success

WHAT IS THE *KEY* TO SUCCESS AT GOLF, GARY?

CONCENTRATION — CONFIDENCE — POSITIVE THINKING — A HEALTHY BODY — A GOOD REPETITIVE SWING. THERE ARE MANY KEYS, TOM!

I WOULD SAY, HOWEVER, THAT GOOD PUTTING IS ESSENTIAL. WHEN YOU PUTT WELL, YOU *CAPITALIZE* ON YOUR GOOD DRIVES, YOUR GOOD APPROACH SHOTS, YOUR GOOD BUNKER SHOTS

YOU MAKE THE MOST OF ALL THAT HAS GONE BEFORE, EVEN IF THAT ONLY MEANS MAKING THE BEST OF A BAD JOB!

WHEN THE PUTTS DROP, THIS HAS A BENEFICIAL EFFECT ON *EVERY DEPARTMENT* OF YOUR GAME. YOUR CONFIDENCE SOARS, YOUR FEARS DIMINISH. CONSEQUENTLY, YOU SWING THE CLUB WITH MORE *AUTHORITY* AND *BETTER CONTROL*

Have a lesson

The best grip

The grip test

Check your calluses!

Don't be a strangler

A relaxing grip

Change your grip

The professional stance

Stand square

Bend your elbow

Arms together

The left wrist

Correct posture

The perfect stance

The shoulder drop

Feet too far apart

Positioning the ball

Try this test

Avoid the corkscrew

Don't over-extend

The correct stance

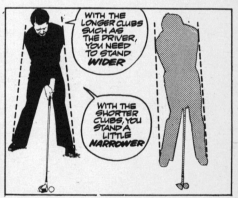

Stand correctly

Don't be a statue

A narrower stance

The position of the feet

Two bad faults

Reserve your energy

Don't be rigid

Sit down

Don't lose your height

An optical illusion

Ground the club correctly

The floor test

How to break tension

17

The position of the hands

Waggle correctly

Starting the back swing

Don't drag the club

18

The correct wrist-break

Hands still

Lock your wrists

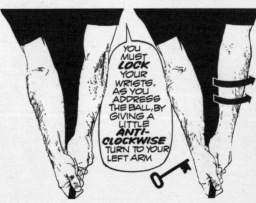

Smooth and passive

The backswing arc

Stretch your muscles

Don't go too far

Don't fall back

Don't swing too far

Reduce your loop

Stay loose

21

Aim at the target

Foot trouble

Don't cut across the line

Club points to target

Inside not outside

Don't go outside

The slow forearm

Increase your arc

The wrist-break

The ideal start

Check your takeaway

Bent legs—the reason why!

Keep in the plane

Slow back for power

The correct plane

Turn—don't tilt

Point to the target

Look for the wrinkles

The correct wrist position

Locked wrists

Open, square or shut?

Do the natural thing

Stay on line

Play the Scottish way

27

Hands last!

How to hit late

Delay the hit

A key move

Hand and knee together

Punch your weight

Don't waste your power

Starting the downswing

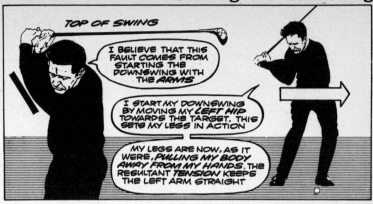

Automatic weight transference

Bent like a bow

Delaying the right shoulder

The power-boost

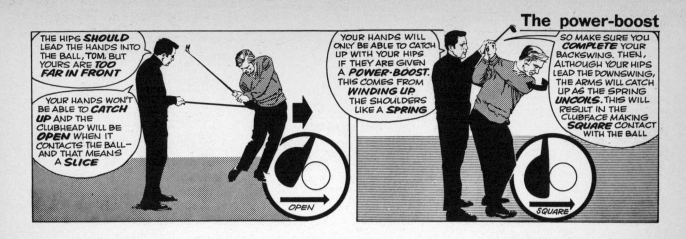
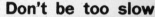

Don't be too slow

Don't lift your heel

Speed on the downswing

31

Leverage

WRONG

BECAUSE YOUR SHOULDERS ARE HORIZONTAL AS YOU START DOWN, IAIN, YOU DO NOT GET THE AMOUNT OF *LEVERAGE* THAT IS NECESSARY TO HIT THE BALL A LONG WAY

CORRECT

TO GET MAXIMUM LEVERAGE USING A POLE, YOU GRIP IT AT ITS *END*, NOT IN THE MIDDLE! SIMILARLY, TO GET FULL LEVERAGE ON THE DOWNSWING, YOU MUST USE THE PART OF YOUR BODY *FURTHEST FROM THE CLUBHEAD* WHICH IS THE *LEFT SHOULDER*

AS YOU START DOWN, GET YOUR LEFT SHOULDER *RISING UP*. THIS WILL *DELAY* THE CLUBHEAD, AND GIVE YOU FAR MORE LEVERAGE

The important right arm

WRONG

YOU ARE ALLOWING YOUR RIGHT ARM TO *BEND* IMMEDIATELY YOU STRIKE THE BALL, TOM

BY DOING SO, YOU LOSE *DISTANCE* AND *ACCURACY*

A STRAIGHT RIGHT ARM AS YOU *HIT THROUGH* THE BALL IS EVERY BIT AS IMPORTANT AS A STRAIGHT LEFT ARM ON THE *BACKSWING*

CORRECT

Stop slicing

THE BASIC CAUSE OF YOUR SLICE, IAIN, IS *POOR HAND ACTION*

WRONG

YOUR HANDS ARE NOT *WORKING* IN THE HITTING AREA

THE BACK OF YOUR LEFT HAND IS FACING THE HOLE LONG AFTER IT SHOULD. THE HANDS MUST *TURN ANTI-CLOCKWISE* AS THEY WHIP THROUGH THE BALL

CORRECT

YOU CAN ENCOURAGE YOUR HANDS TO WORK BY STANDING *OPEN* ON THE PRACTICE TEE AND TRYING TO HIT THE BALL *STRAIGHT*

OPEN

IT REQUIRES VERY GOOD HAND ACTION TO SQUARE UP THE CLUBHEAD, AS THE NATURAL TENDENCY WITH THIS STANCE IS FOR THE HEAD TO BE OPEN AT IMPACT

You must release

FAILURE TO COCK THE WRISTS ON THE BACKSWING, TOM, PREVENTS YOU FROM *RELEASING YOUR POWER* IN THE HITTING AREA

THE RESULT IS A *WEAK* SHOT

WHEN THE WRISTS ARE PROPERLY COCKED, THEY ARE READY TO *RELEASE* YOUR POWER

YOU GET A TREMENDOUS FOLLOW-THROUGH, WITH FURTHER COCKING OF THE WRISTS INDICATING THAT YOU HAVE *RELEASED* THROUGH THE BALL

Supinate the wrists

Impact and follow-through

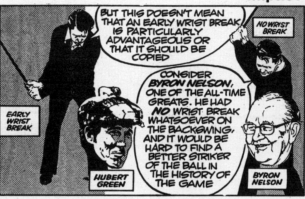

Don't be wooden

Don't change planes

How to hit solidly

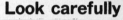

Look carefully

The key to extension

Improve your leg action

How to transfer your weight

Don't back away

Don't roll too soon

Stay down

Stay behind the ball

How to stop swaying

Three things to remember

Pigeon toes

How to finish

The essential follow-through

The important follow-through

Use your body

Two important thoughts

Swing within yourself

Check your swing

Visualize a perfect swing

Tempo-two key moves

Smooth and rhythmic

Don't stop at the top

Developing tempo

Dont "snatch"

The knee-kick

Slicing and hooking

Women—stand tall

Toe, heel and center!

Winter Rules

Up-slopes, down-slopes

Hit it cleanly

section two
The Tee Shot

Control your nerves

Chase after the ball

High tee for Arnie

Two essential actions

Tee up correctly

The long drive

When to shorten your grip

Don't be a square!

Be a straight-shooter

Stand tall

Use your weight correctly

Where to tee up

Tee up with care

Legs for distance

45

How to swing wide

Relax for distance

How to drive further

On narrow fairways . . .

section three
Fairway Shots

Conquer your nerves

I *TOPPED* IT, GARY! JUST WHEN I HAD A GREAT CHANCE TO WIN A HOLE!

THANKS FOR LETTING ME OFF THE HOOK, TOM

WHEN YOU ARE IN A *TENSE* POSITION, YOU MUST NOT LET YOUR *NERVES* BEAT YOU

IF I HAVE A MAKE-OR-BREAK SHOT TO PLAY, I REMIND MYSELF OF TWO VITAL COMPONENTS OF THE SWING. *HEAD DOWN* AND *FOLLOW THROUGH*

HEAD DOWN

IF I DO THESE TWO THINGS, THE CHANCES ARE THE SHOT WILL WORK OUT FINE— DESPITE THE *PRESSURE*

FOLLOW THROUGH

Forward and back!

I CAN'T GET MY SHOTS UP IN THE AIR TODAY, GARY!

YOUR WHOLE BODY IS *LEANING FORWARD* AS YOU HIT THROUGH, IAIN. THAT IS CAUSING YOU TO *SMOTHER* THE BALL

TO GET DECENT HEIGHT ON THE BALL, THE *BOTTOM* PART OF YOUR BODY MUST GO *FORWARD* WHILE THE *TOP* PART *STAYS BACK*

TOM WEISKOPF AND *TOMMY BOLT* DO THIS BETTER THAN ANYONE ELSE I CAN THINK OF

Mastering the fairway woods

Don't "top" your fairway woods

Watch it fly

Trust the clubface

The long irons

Long iron trouble

A five second tip

Place your ball

section four
The Wedge Shot

Mastering the wedge

GARY, WHY IS IT THAT MOST WEEKEND GOLFERS ARE POOR *WEDGE* PLAYERS—LIKE ME?

THERE ARE SEVERAL REASONS, TOM

BUT, IF I HAD TO PICK OUT *ONE*, I'D SAY IT'S BECAUSE THEY TAKE THE CLUB BACK IN *ONE PIECE*

WRONG

THIS IS CORRECT FOR THE *DRIVER* AND THE *LONGER CLUBS*, BUT *DEAD WRONG* FOR THE WEDGE

FOR *ALL* WEDGE SHOTS, *BREAK THE WRISTS QUICKLY* ON THE TAKEAWAY

Be crisp

THE *WEDGE* SHOT MUST BE *CRISP* AND AUTHORITATIVE, TOM

WRONG

YOUR FOLLOW-THROUGH IS LONG AND SLOPPY, YOUR ARMS ARE *BENT*, YOUR RIGHT LEG IS *STRAIGHT* AND YOUR *HEAD* HAS MOVED FORWARD

CORRECT

MY *HEAD* IS ACTUALLY *BEHIND* WHERE THE BALL WAS SITTING. MY FOLLOW-THROUGH IS FAIRLY SHORT AND MY *ARMS* ARE *STRAIGHT*. MY *RIGHT KNEE* IS *BENT* IN TOWARDS THE TARGET AND MY WEIGHT IS ON MY *LEFT FOOT*

An extra wedge

A matter of feel

Softly does it

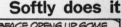

The half shot

Grip short

Waggle correctly

Hands up

Don't look up!

How to get backspin

Don't chip

Stay relaxed

The professional approach

Perfect pitch

The importance of knees

The wedge to the green

Pitching over a mound

section five
Sand Shots

Rhythm is the keyword

YOU MUST NEVER *QUIT* ON THE SHOT, TOM, PARTICULARLY WHEN PLAYING OUT OF SAND

MANY WEEKEND GOLFERS ARE SO TIMID IN BUNKERS THAT THEY HARDLY HAVE ANY FOLLOW-THROUGH AT ALL

FOR ALL BUNKER SHOTS TAKE A FAIRLY *BIG BACKSWING* AND *FOLLOW RIGHT THROUGH*

PROVIDED YOU *CUT THROUGH THE SAND* UNDERNEATH THE BALL, YOU WON'T HAVE TO WORRY ABOUT HITTING TOO FAR

RHYTHM IS THE KEYWORD WHEN PLAYING FROM SAND — IF YOUR SWING IS *SHORT* AND *JERKY*, THE BALL WILL GO NOWHERE

Gripping short

FOR *ALL* BUNKER SHOTS, YOU SHOULD GRIP THE CLUB *SHORT*, TOM

GRIPPING SHORT

THIS GIVES YOU A LITTLE BIT OF *EXTRA CONTROL*

I DON'T CARE IF IT'S DOWNSLOPE, UPSLOPE, SIDE-SLOPE OR WHATEVER — SLIDE YOUR HANDS DOWN THE SHAFT A BIT

YOU WILL DEFINITELY GET BETTER *"FEEL"*

Avoid the sand

Watch where you look!

Reading the sand

Plugged in the sand

A change of club

I NEVER GET THESE *LONG BUNKER SHOTS* UP TO THE HOLE, GARY!

TRY MY CLUB, TOM, AND SWING IN EXACTLY THE SAME WAY

THAT'S *AMAZING*, GARY, I DIDN'T HIT ANY *HARDER* YET I'VE REACHED THE HOLE

NOT SO AMAZING, TOM! THE CLUB I GAVE YOU IS A *WEDGE* WHICH HAS LESS LOFT THAN A *SAND-WEDGE*

I FIND IT IS A MUCH MORE SATISFACTORY CLUB FOR THE *LONG* BUNKER SHOT WHICH IS THE *HARDEST* SHOT IN GOLF

Chipping from sand

NORMALLY, AS YOU KNOW, TOM I WOULDN'T DREAM OF *CHIPPING* OUT OF A BUNKER. BUT HERE IS ONE TIME WHEN I MIGHT JUST DO SO

THIS IS A *LONG* BUNKER SHOT (THE FLAG IS ALL OF 35 YARDS AWAY) AND THERE IS *NOT MUCH OF A LIP* TO GET OVER

ALL MY WEIGHT IS ON MY LEFT SIDE. I ADDRESS THE BALL OPPOSITE MY *RIGHT BIG TOE* WITH MY LEFT ARM MORE OR LESS IN LINE WITH MY LEFT LEG

I CERTAINLY DON'T WANT TO CATCH THE *SAND* FIRST—THAT WOULD KILL THE SHOT

THIS STANCE ENSURES THAT I HIT THE BALL CLEANLY

Flick the clubhead

I NEVER GET THESE *LONG BUNKER SHOTS* UP TO THE HOLE, GARY!

YOU MAKE *TWO* BASIC MISTAKES, TOM

FAULT 1

YOU ADDRESS THE BALL OPPOSITE YOUR *LEFT* FOOT

AND YOU *QUIT* ON THE SHOT. THE RESULT IS THAT THE BALL COMES OUT TOO *HIGH*

QUIT

FAULT 2

WITH A LONG BUNKER SHOT, A *LOW TRAJECTORY* IS REQUIRED. THEREFORE, I ADDRESS THE BALL IN THE *CENTER* OF MY FEET

SNAP

I ALSO *FLICK* THE CLUBHEAD AT THE BALL IN A *POSITIVE, CRISP* MANNER. I WANT TO FEEL THE CLUBHEAD *SNAP* THROUGH THE SAND INTO A *GOOD FOLLOW-THROUGH*

The long bunker shot

WHEN PLAYING A *LONG* BUNKER SHOT, IAIN, I GRIP THE CLUB *CONSIDERABLY SHORTER* THAN I DO ON THE FAIRWAY

THIS COMPENSATES FOR THE FACT THAT MY HANDS ARE *CLOSER* TO THE BALL BECAUSE MY FEET ARE *DUG DOWN* INTO THE SAND FOR A *SECURE STANCE*

I AIM FOR THE *TOP* OF THE BALL AND TRY TO HIT IT THERE BECAUSE A *CLEAN HIT* IS ESSENTIAL. IF THE CLUB STRIKES THE *SAND* FIRST, I'VE GOT NO CHANCE OF REACHING THE GREEN

Play a chop shot

Play safe

section six
Chipping

How I practise chipping

WHEN I AM PRACTISING MY CHIPPING, I DIVIDE THE BALLS INTO THREE LOTS ABOUT A YARD APART

USING THE SAME CLUB THROUGHOUT, I HIT A *LOW* CHIP FROM LOT ONE, A MEDIUM CHIP FROM LOT TWO THEN A HIGH CHIP FROM LOT THREE.

I THEN HIT A MEDIUM CHIP FROM LOT ONE, A HIGH CHIP FROM LOT TWO AND A LOW CHIP FROM LOT THREE

BY PLAYING A VARIETY OF SHOTS LIKE THIS, MY HANDS ARE TRAINED TO DEAL WITH VARYING CONDITIONS. MY *MUSCLE MEMORY* AND SENSE OF *"FEEL"* ARE GREATLY IMPROVED

The Texas wedge

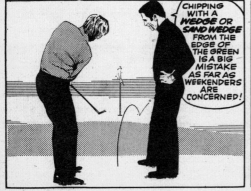

CHIPPING WITH A *WEDGE* OR *SAND WEDGE* FROM THE EDGE OF THE GREEN IS A BIG MISTAKE AS FAR AS WEEKENDERS ARE CONCERNED!

WHEN YOU HAVE TO GO OVER A *MOUND*, YOU WILL GET MORE CONSISTENT RESULTS WITH A *PUTTER*, ESPECIALLY WHEN THE GREEN IS *HARD* AND THE FLAG IS AT THE *FRONT*

IF YOU *PRACTISE* THOSE *TEXAS WEDGE* SHOTS OVER MOUNDS, IAIN, YOUR SCORING IS BOUND TO IMPROVE

Putt for safety

Practice with a purpose

How to chip well

Complete the shot

Chipping check

Chip like Arnie

Pitch it closer

Chipping downhill

Allow for the slope

Short back—long through

Better chipping

Two aids to chipping

Ban the wedge

The important chip shot

Chipping over a bunker

The run-up chip

A running chip

Uhill and downhill chips

Poor chippers—try this!

Head down

Accurate chipping

Chip with your knees

Rhythmic chipping

The run-up chip

Try blinkers

The chipping secret

Two aids to chipping

Don't use a putter

Chipping practice

The correct attitude

A chipping lesson

Beware wet grass

Wet greens

Chipping from long grass

Play safe

Chipping from sand

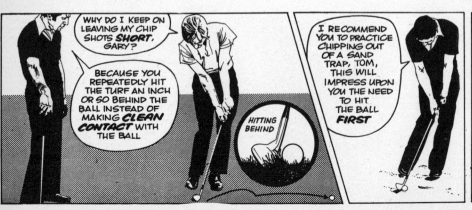

section seven
Putting

The basics of putting

Why reverse overlap?

A repeating putting stroke

THE BIG THING ABOUT PUTTING, TOM, IS TO FIND A STROKE THAT WORKS FOR *YOU*

IT IS IMPOSSIBLE TO SAY WHAT THE RIGHT STROKE IS. *BOBBY LOCKE* USED TO AIM TO THE *RIGHT*, TAKE THE PUTTER BACK ON THE INSIDE, AND *HOOK* THE BALL IN, WHEREAS *FLORY VAN DONCK* OF *BELGIUM* HAD THE TOE OF THE PUTTER 'WAY OFF THE GROUND

SO REALLY THE PUTTING ACTION DOESN'T MATTER ALL THAT MUCH

WHAT IS IMPORTANT IS TO HAVE A *REPEATING* PUTTING STROKE — ONE THAT IS THE SAME DAY IN DAY OUT. AND THAT TAKES HOURS OF *PRACTICE*

Like a pendulum

ON LONG PUTTS, A *SHORT* BACKSWING WILL PRODUCE A *CHOPPY* STROKE LACKING IN SMOOTH *TEMPO*

FOR PUTTS *OVER 15 FEET*, THE BLADE MUST BE TAKEN BACK *PAST THE RIGHT LEG*

THIS WILL PRODUCE A KIND OF SMOOTH, *PENDULUM* ACTION WHICH WILL SET THE BALL ROLLING TO THE HOLE WITH *TOPSPIN*

Try a little kick

TWO FAULTS, IAIN. YOU ARE TAKING THE PUTTER BACK *OUTSIDE* THE LINE, AND YOU ARE NOT *FOLLOWING-THROUGH*!

YOU CAN LEARN A LOT ABOUT THE MECHANICS OF PUTTING IF YOU TRY TO ROLL THE BALL INTO THE HOLE WITH YOUR *FOOT*

YOU WILL FIND THAT YOU TAKE YOUR FOOT BACK ON THE *INSIDE* EVERY TIME

ALSO, YOU WILL *FOLLOW-THROUGH* EVERY TIME. THESE ARE TWO *VITAL* INGREDIENTS OF GOOD PUTTING

A change of address

I'VE MISSED SIX TIDDLERS TODAY, GARY!

I DON'T LIKE THE WAY YOU *ADDRESS* THOSE SHORT PUTTS, IAIN!

YOU STAND FAR TOO *UPRIGHT*, AND YOU GRIP THE PUTTER TOO NEAR THE END OF THE SHAFT

I BEND MY BACK AND GRIP THE CLUB *VERY SHORT*

THIS HELPS ME TO KEEP MY PUTTING STROKE *FIRM* AND *COMPACT*. THERE IS LESS CHANCE OF MY PUTTER *WOBBLING* DURING THE SWING

Check your alignment

Experiment!

Front or back?

Don't change your mind

A great stroke-saver

Long and slow

Break for long putts

Never be careless

Improve your putting

Vary your backswing

Putt like Nicklaus

Hands down

Don't take too long

YOU'RE TAKING *AGES* OVER YOUR PUTTS TODAY, IAIN

I KNOW I AM, GARY. MY PUTTING'S GONE RIGHT OFF

THE WORST THING YOU CAN DO IS TO TAKE TOO LONG OVER A PUTT. ALL YOU DO IS BUILD UP *EXTRA TENSION* AND KEEP CHANGING YOUR MIND

WHEN YOUR PUTTING STARTS TO LET YOU DOWN, IT IS FAR BETTER TO *REDUCE* THE LENGTH OF TIME YOU TAKE OVER THE PUTT, AND STRIKE THE PUTT CONFIDENTLY BEFORE YOUR NERVES GET A CHANCE TO UPSET YOU

The putting mystery

I'VE BEEN PUTTING FAIRLY WELL FOR A MONTH, GARY— NOW I CAN'T HOLE A THING!

PUTTING IS A GAME IN ITSELF, TOM. IT IS FULL OF *MYSTERY*

OFTEN OUR SUCCESSES AND OUR FAILURES ARE ENTIRELY DUE TO OUR *STATE OF MIND*. ONE DAY WE ARE THINKING RIGHT, THE NEXT, WE ARE NOT

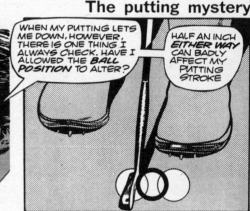

WHEN MY PUTTING LETS ME DOWN, HOWEVER, THERE IS ONE THING I ALWAYS CHECK. HAVE I ALLOWED THE *BALL POSITION* TO ALTER?

HALF AN INCH *EITHER WAY* CAN BADLY AFFECT MY PUTTING STROKE

Which hand?

WHICH HAND SHOULD I STRIKE THE PUTT WITH, GARY?

THE ONE WHICH HAS THE MOST "*FEEL*", TOM

IN YOUR CASE, IT'S OBVIOUSLY THE LEFT HAND, BECAUSE THAT'S THE ONE YOU COLLECT THE BETS WITH!

WHEN SOMEONE IS HANDED A DOLLAR BILL, HE INVARIABLY TAKES IT WITH THE HAND WHICH HAS THE GREATER SENSE OF "*FEEL*"

I HAVE BETTER "*FEEL*" IN MY RIGHT HAND, SO I LET IT INITIATE THE STRIKING ACTION

Practice long putts

YOU'RE NOT GETTING YOUR *LONG* PUTTS UP TO THE HOLE, TOM. THIS IS TYPICAL OF THE GOLFER WHO ONLY PLAYS ON *WEEKENDS*

YOU ADDRESS THE BALL TOO FAR BACK WHEREAS I HAVE IT OPPOSITE MY *LEFT* TOE

THIS HELPS ME TO HAVE A *SMOOTH* STROKE AND A *LONGER STROKE*. I, THEREFORE, GET MORE *TOPSPIN* ON THE BALL WHICH GIVES ME MORE *FEEL*

WEEKENDERS HARDLY EVER PRACTICE *LONG* PUTTS. THIS IS A PITY BECAUSE, IF YOU CAN KNOCK IT UP *CLOSE*, YOU WON'T MISS NEARLY SO MANY *SHORT* PUTTS!

Training matches

A good putting habit

The painted putter

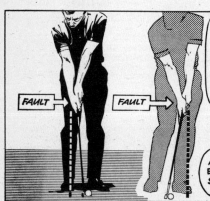

Drop your shoulder

A repeating stroke

The master hand

Change your putter

Be consistent

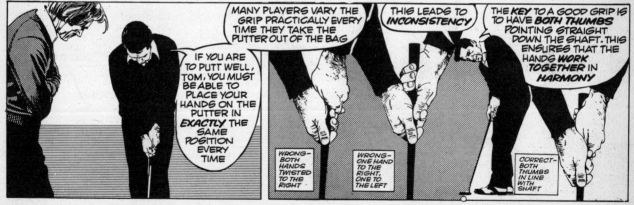

Save strokes—speed up play

Don't be timid

Head still

Checking the grain

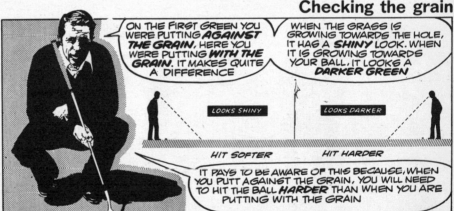

Long or short?

Use a glove

Open the blade

How to stop jabbing

Don't hook your putts

79

Conquer your nerves

I NEEDED THAT *2-FOOTER* FOR A BIRDIE, GARY!

YOUR *NERVES* GOT THE BETTER OF YOU, TOM! YOU WERE *LOOKING* AT THE HOLE BEFORE YOU MADE CONTACT WITH THE BALL!

THIS PUT THE CLUBHEAD FRACTIONALLY *OUT OF LINE* WHICH WAS SUFFICIENT TO MAKE YOU MISS THE PUTT!

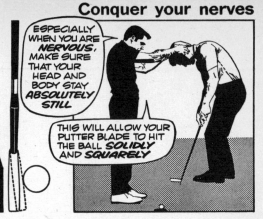

ESPECIALLY WHEN YOU ARE *NERVOUS,* MAKE SURE THAT YOUR HEAD AND BODY STAY *ABSOLUTELY STILL*

THIS WILL ALLOW YOUR PUTTER BLADE TO HIT THE BALL *SOLIDLY* AND *SQUARELY*

Shorten your swing

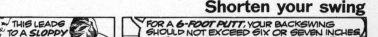

THIS LEADS TO A SLOPPY STROKE WHICH HAS NO *FIRMNESS* OR *AUTHORITY*

GARY— WHY DO I MISS SO MANY *6-FOOT PUTTS?*

BECAUSE YOU TAKE THE PUTTER *TOO FAR BACK,* TOM

FOR A *6-FOOT PUTT,* YOUR BACKSWING SHOULD NOT EXCEED SIX OR SEVEN INCHES. THIS WILL ENSURE THAT YOUR STROKE HAS *CRISPNESS*

A GOOD WAY TO PRACTICE THIS IS TO PLACE AN OBJECT SIX INCHES BEHIND YOU WHICH WILL *AUTOMATICALLY LIMIT YOUR BACKSWING*

Coping with fast greens

THESE GREENS ARE LIKE *LIGHTNING,* GARY!

WELL, YOU'D BETTER STOP *CHARGING* THE BALL UP TO THE HOLE, TOM

WHEN YOU HIT YOUR PUTT *HARD,* YOU ONLY HAVE *ONE CHANCE* OF SINKING IT. THE BALL HAS GOT TO HIT THE *BACK* OF THE HOLE AND DROP IN

BUT THERE ARE *FOUR* WAYS IN, PROVIDED YOU COAX YOUR BALL *GENTLY* TO THE HOLE

A SLOW BALL CAN GO IN AT THE *FRONT* OR TRICKLE ITS WAY ROUND THE HOLE, DROPPING IN AT ONE OF THE *SIDE-DOORS* OR EVEN AT THE *BACK*

The pistol grip

MY PUTTING IS VERY INCONSISTENT, GARY

SO IS THE POSITION OF YOUR *LEFT HAND.* IT CHANGES ALL THE TIME. THE *LEFT THUMB* MUST *ALWAYS* BE STRAIGHT DOWN THE SHAFT

BAD

BAD

MY PUTTER HAS A SPECIALLY SHAPED *PISTOL GRIP* WHICH ENSURES THAT I HOLD THE CLUB THE *SAME WAY* EVERY TIME WITH MY THUMB STRAIGHT DOWN THE SHAFT

GET YOUR PRO TO FIT ONE ON YOUR PUTTER—IT WILL MAKE A GREAT DIFFERENCE TO YOUR PUTTING STROKE

CORRECT

Don't jab

FOLLOW-THROUGH, TOM! DON'T *JAB* YOUR PUTTS!

BUT WHEN I CONSCIOUSLY FOLLOW-THROUGH, GARY, IT DOESN'T *FEEL* RIGHT!

PUTTER STOPS

IT FEELS UNNATURAL BECAUSE YOUR SET-UP IS WRONG. YOUR *RIGHT SHOULDER IS TOO HIGH*, YOUR RIGHT ARM TOO STRAIGHT AND YOUR WEIGHT IS TOO MUCH ON YOUR *LEFT SIDE*

YOU MUST *DROP* YOUR SHOULDER AND MOVE SOME OF YOUR WEIGHT BACK ON TO THE RIGHT FOOT SO THAT YOUR WEIGHT ONLY SLIGHTLY FAVORS YOUR LEFT SIDE

THE PUTTER WILL NOW SLIDE THROUGH *NATURALLY*, AND IT WILL BE *IMPOSSIBLE* TO JAB THE BALL

Putting practice

YARDS *SHORT*, GARY. I'M GOING TO 3-PUTT AGAIN

TAKE *SIX* BALLS AND PLACE THEM ROUND THE GREEN — AS FAR FROM THE HOLE AS POSSIBLE

1. 2° 3° 4°
5. 6.

WHEN WE'VE COMPLETED THIS ROUND, TOM, I'LL SHOW...

NOW, WHAT YOU HAVE TO DO IS GET DOWN IN *TWO* FROM EACH POSITION. THE MOMENT YOU FAIL TO DO SO YOU GO BACK TO THE *BEGINNING* AND START AGAIN

SHORT-START AGAIN

ALSO — IF YOU LEAVE AN APPROACH PUTT *SHORT* OF THE HOLE YOU GO BACK TO THE BEGINNING. IT'S TOUGH — BUT IT TEACHES YOU TO GET THE BALL *UP TO THE HOLE* AND TO *CONCENTRATE* ON EACH SHOT!

Marking your ball

SOME PEOPLE PLACE IT IN *FRONT* THEN, WHEN THEY REPLACE THE BALL, THEY PUT THE BALL IN *FRONT* OF THE COIN. THIS IS AN ILLEGAL WAY OF GAINING A COUPLE OF INCHES.

ILLEGAL → TO HOLE

ON A SHORT PUTT, A TWO-INCH ADVANTAGE CAN BE QUITE HELPFUL. BUT DON'T RISK IT — IF YOUR OPPONENT COMPLAINS, IT CAN COST YOU THE HOLE.

Fringe putting

I'M ALWAYS *SHORT* WHEN I USE MY PUTTER FROM OFF THE GREEN, GARY!

WHEN PUTTING FROM THE FRINGE, TOM, I ALWAYS TRY TO GET MY BALL UP TO AN *IMAGINARY HOLE* THREE FEET BEYOND THE REAL HOLE

BY STRIKING THE PUTT JUST THAT *LITTLE BIT HARDER* IT MAKES UP FOR THE FACT THAT THE FRINGE GRASS TAKES SOME OF THE *PACE* OFF THE BALL

81

Beware damp greens

Learn from your successes

Forget the clubhead

Don't be short

Never quit

YOU ARE *QUITTING* ON THE PUTT, TOM. THE CLUBHEAD IS *SLOWING DOWN* THE MOMENT IT STRIKES THE BALL

THE CLUBHEAD MUST *ACCELERATE* THROUGH THE BALL. THIS APPLIES TO *EVERY* SHOT YOU PLAY ON THE GOLF COURSE

ACCELERATE

KEEP THE BACK OF YOUR LEFT HAND MOVING THROUGH ALONG THE TARGET LINE FOR *ACCURACY* AND *CONTROL*

A simple putting tip

DO YOU KNOW WHY YOU MISSED THAT 3-FOOTER, TOM?

NO!

SIMPLY BECAUSE OF *TENSION*. THE VEINS WERE STANDING OUT ON YOUR NECK AND HANDS, AND YOUR TEETH WERE CLENCHED

YOU CAN RELEASE THIS TENSION BY *EXHALING YOUR BREATH* JUST BEFORE YOU MAKE YOUR PUTTING STROKE

THIS SIMPLE TIP CAN WORK WONDERS ON THE GREEN

Keep to the line

IF A PUTT BREAKS FROM RIGHT-TO-LEFT, GARY, I NEARLY ALWAYS MISS IT ON THE *LEFT*, AND VICE VERSA.

THIS IS BECAUSE YOU TEND TO *HOOK* THE RIGHT-TO-LEFT PUTTS AND *PUSH* THE LEFT-TO-RIGHT ONES.

IN THE ONE YOU JUST MISSED, YOU KNEW THAT YOU HAD TO KEEP YOUR BLADE GOING THROUGH TO THE RIGHT OF THE HOLE . . .

. . . BUT YOU WERE TOO "HOLE CONSCIOUS". YOUR HANDS TURNED INSTINCTIVELY TOWARDS IT.

ONCE YOU'VE *CHOSEN* THE LINE, HAVE THE CONFIDENCE TO *KEEP* TO IT.

A terrible crime

AW — LOOK AT THAT, GARY! SIX INCHES SHORT!

THAT IS ONE OF THE BIGGEST *CRIMES* IN GOLF, TOM

YOU SHOULD NEVER BE *SHORT!* GET YOUR PUTTS *PAST* THE HOLE, WHATEVER ELSE YOU DO!

OBVIOUSLY THIS GIVES THE BALL A *CHANCE* TO GO IN, BUT THERE IS *MORE* TO IT THAN THAT

PSYCHOLOGICALLY, YOU BENEFIT FROM BEING THAT LITTLE BIT *BOLDER*

IT CREATES A *POSITIVE ATTITUDE* OF MIND WHICH IS *ABSOLUTELY ESSENTIAL* IN GOLF. PERSONALLY, I AM MORE CONFIDENT OF SINKING A BALL THAT IS FOUR FEET *PAST* THE HOLE THAN ONE THAT HAS STOPPED FOUR FEET SHORT

All putts are straight

Do something different

Avoid the heel

Try a 3-iron

Vary your practice

A sloping 6-footer

Mind the fringe

Local knowledge

section eight
Course Strategy

A carbon copy

YOU HIT THAT SHOT WITHOUT FIRST HAVING A *PRACTICE SWING*, TOM

NO PROFESSIONAL GOLFER WOULD EVER DO THAT. THE PRACTICE SWING IS A VERY NECESSARY *PRELUDE* WHICH SHOULD NEVER BE NEGLECTED

IT IS A WAY OF *PREPARING* YOURSELF FOR THE SHOT YOU WANT TO EXECUTE AND OF TELLING YOUR *MUSCLES* WHAT YOU WANT THEM TO DO

THE PRACTICE SWING SHOULD ALWAYS BE A *CARBON COPY* OF THE ACTUAL SHOT WHICH YOU MEAN TO PLAY

Don't get tense

BY PLACING YOUR CLUBHEAD BEHIND THE BALL *BEFORE* STARTING TO LOOK AT THE HOLE, YOU BUILD UP TENSION IN YOUR *ARMS*, IAIN!

I KEEP MY ARMS NICE AND *RELAXED* WHILE I MAKE UP MY MIND HOW TO PLAY THE HOLE

THIS ADVICE IS PARTICULARLY IMPORTANT TO NOT-SO-YOUNG GOLFERS AND THOSE WHO HAVE A TENDENCY TO BE *STIFF*

Improve your concentration

IT IS NOT ENOUGH TO HAVE A GOOD GOLFSWING, IAIN. *CONCENTRATION* IS EQUALLY IMPORTANT

I HAVE THREE WAYS OF KEEPING MY MIND ON THE GAME. ONE, I PACE OUT EVERY DRIVE I HIT

TWO, AS I WALK TO THE GREENS, I LOOK AT THE BUNKERS AND TRY TO JUDGE HOW FAR EACH ONE IS FROM THE FLAG

THREE, WHEN I STEP ONTO THE GREEN, I STUDY THE *GRAIN* AND LOOK FOR *HIDDEN SLOPES*

THIS KIND OF ROUTINE PREVENTS THE MIND GOING OFF AT A TANGENT

Get out of trouble

LOOK AT THAT, GARY! IT'S JUST ONE BAD SHOT AFTER ANOTHER!

TOM, I'M GOING TO GIVE YOU A SIMPLE PIECE OF ADVICE THAT IS REALLY *VERY VALUABLE*

WHEN A HIGH-HANDICAP PLAYER GETS INTO *ANY KIND* OF TROUBLE, HE SHOULD HAVE *ONE THOUGHT* IN MIND AND THAT IS TO *GET BACK ONTO THE FAIRWAY* EVEN IF IT MEANS PLAYING OUT *SIDEWAYS*

DESPAIR · CONFUSION · ANGER · DOUBTS

NOT ONLY HAVE YOU *WASTED* STROKES, YOU HAVE DISTURBED YOUR MIND AND SET UP A MENTAL CONFLICT WITHIN YOU WHICH CAN AFFECT THE REST OF THE ROUND

IF YOU GO IN THE ROUGH THEN HOOK INTO THE TREES AS YOU DID, IT HAS A VERY BAD *PSYCHOLOGICAL EFFECT*

Play the course correctly

YOU MUST PLAY THE COURSE SENSIBLY, IAIN. IT'S SILLY TO *CUT* YOUR TEE SHOT ON A DOG-LEG LEFT. YOU'RE ONLY GETTING FURTHER AWAY FROM THE HOLE

PLAY THE COURSE THE WAY IT'S DESIGNED, ON A DOG-LEG LEFT, *HOOK* YOUR TEE SHOT

ON A DOG-LEG RIGHT, *SLICE* YOUR DRIVE. SO MANY PEOPLE GET INTO TROUBLE BY TACKLING THESE HOLES THE *WRONG WAY ROUND*

CLOSED STANCE

OPEN STANCE

Cutting the corner

A *DOG-LEG* TO THE RIGHT, TOM. ARE YOU GOING TO CUT THE CORNER?

I'D LIKE TO, GARY, BUT I CAN'T BE SURE THE BALL WILL *SLICE* WHEN I WANT IT TO!

IT'S NOT SO DIFFICULT, TOM. JUST TAKE THE CLUB BACK TO *11 O'CLOCK*

AND SWING IT THROUGH TO *5 O'CLOCK*

11

6

6

5

THAT WILL PRODUCE THE CLASSIC *OUT-TO-IN* SWING WHICH PUTS *CLOCKWISE SPIN* ON THE BALL

87

Drive for position

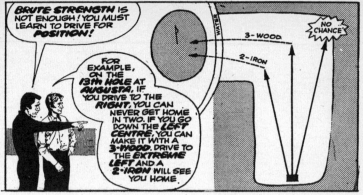

One positive thought

Forget the flag

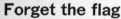

A great stroke-saver

The right approach

Think before you play

The professional attitude

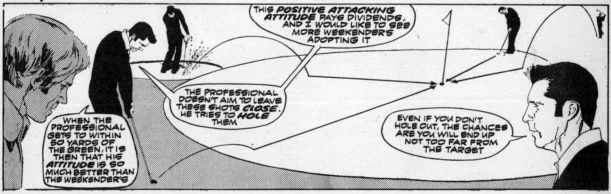

Think!

Three ways to success

Be optimistic

Safety first

Be a thinker

90

Play the correct shot

The importance of good eyes

Choose carefully

Be alert

Fair pin positions

Hit higher

Don't go for the flag

Increase your backspin

Approaching hard greens

IT'S NOT EASY TO STOP YOUR BALL WHEN THE GROUND IS *BAKED HARD* WITH THE SUN, TOM!

I'VE GONE RIGHT THROUGH THE GREEN, GARY!

THE BEST THING TO DO IN THESE CONDITIONS IS TO HIT THE BALL *HIGH*. REMEMBER, YOU GET MORE HEIGHT WITH ANY CLUB THE *HARDER* YOU HIT THE SHOT!

SO, TAKE ONE CLUB *LESS* THAN YOU WOULD NORMALLY TAKE AND HIT THE BALL *HARD*. A HARD *9-IRON* WILL GO AS FAR AS A NORMAL *8-IRON*.

ARNOLD PALMER DID THIS AT THE PAR-3 12th HOLE IN THE *U.S. MASTERS* IN 1962 WHEN HE BEAT ME IN THE PLAY-OFF. HE THOUGHT IT WAS A *7-IRON*, SO HE TOOK A FULL *8-IRON* AND STOPPED HIS BALL ON A VERY HARD GREEN.

A break in concentration

I'VE SLICED INTO THE WATER, GARY! THAT TRAIN CAME ALONG AT THE WRONG MOMENT!

WHY DIDN'T YOU WAIT, IAIN?

WHEN SOMETHING DISTURBS YOUR CONCENTRATION, IT'S A MISTAKE TO CONTINUE YOUR SWING

STEP ASIDE — WAIT TILL EVERYTHING IS NORMAL AGAIN — THEN RE-ADDRESS THE BALL

CONCENTRATION IS ONE OF THE ESSENTIAL FACTORS. THE MAN WHO CAN REALLY KEEP HIS MIND ON THE JOB HAS A TREMENDOUS ADVANTAGE

The practice swing

THAT SOFT, EASY PRACTICE SWING IS GOING TO DO YOU NO GOOD AT ALL, TOM

SLOW

IF YOU'RE GOING TO REACH THE GREEN, YOU'LL NEED TO HIT THAT BALL TEN YARDS FURTHER THAN YOU NORMALLY DO WITH A 3-WOOD

QUICK

THEREFORE, MAKE YOUR PRACTICE SWING *HARDER* THAN YOUR ACTUAL SWING. TELL YOUR MUSCLES WHAT IS EXPECTED OF THEM AND *LOOSEN* THEM UP SO THAT YOU WILL GET THE CLUBHEAD SPEED YOU REQUIRE

Play safe

I'M IN TERRIBLE TROUBLE, GARY, YET I ONLY SLICED THAT *3-IRON* SHOT A FEW YARDS OFF LINE.

WITH THE FLAG AT THE *RIGHT*, YOU WERE SILLY TO AIM STRAIGHT FOR IT, TOM.

WHEN A HIGH HANDICAP GOLFER PLAYS A *LONG* OR A *MEDIUM* IRON, HE SHOULD ALWAYS AIM FOR THE *MIDDLE* OF THE GREEN.

THEN, IF THE BALL SLICES OR HOOKS, THERE WILL STILL BE A *CHANCE* IT WILL END ON THE *PUTTING SURFACE*.

Be observant

The last few holes

A narrow fairway

Stay bold

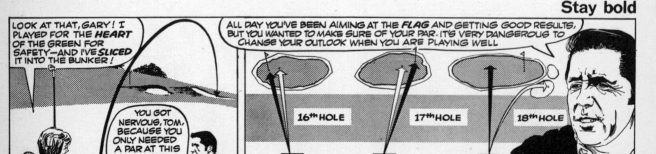

Shoot away from trouble

Remember to change

Be decisive

One shot at a time

Tactical driving

Aiming for trouble

Play to the back

Visualise success

The vital question

I'M GOING THROUGH THIS GAP IN THE TREES STRAIGHT TO THE GREEN, GARY

DO YOU REALLY THINK YOU'RE THAT GOOD, TOM?

ASK YOURSELF THIS QUESTION — WOULD YOU PLAY THIS SHOT FOR A $50 BET?

NO, BUT....

WELL, THERE'S YOUR ANSWER. YOU DON'T *REALLY* THINK YOU HAVE A GOOD CHANCE OF MAKING THE SHOT! SO WHY NOT ADMIT IT AND ATTEMPT SOMETHING THAT IS *WITHIN YOUR CAPABILITIES*?

THE SAFE WAY

Go for the big one

THIS HOLE ALWAYS BUGS ME, GARY. I NEED TO HIT A PRETTY GOOD 3-IRON TO REACH THE GREEN AND, INVARIABLY, I MAKE A MESS OF IT!

I DON'T LIKE TO SEE WEEKENDERS TRYING TO HIT THEIR *LONG-IRONS* FLAT OUT, TOM... IT'S USUALLY DISASTROUS!

THE ANSWER IN A SITUATION LIKE THIS, TOM, IS TO SQUEEZE A FEW *EXTRA YARDS* OUT OF YOUR *TEE SHOT* BY HOOKING THE BALL

THE FAIRWAY IS VERY WIDE AND YOU CAN'T GET INTO ANY BIG TROUBLE IF YOUR DRIVE GOES ASTRAY

HOOKED DRIVE

NORMAL DRIVE

CLOSE YOUR STANCE, TURN YOUR HANDS A LITTLE BIT TO YOUR *RIGHT*, AND LET FLY. IF ALL GOES WELL YOU'LL BE HITTING A 4-IRON OR MAYBE EVEN A 5-IRON TO THE GREEN

HOOKER'S GRIP

Match play

IN MATCH PLAY, THE FIRST TWO HOLES ARE VERY IMPORTANT, TOM

IF YOU CAN GO ON TO THE THIRD TEE ONE OR TWO UP, YOU HAVE A TREMENDOUS *PSYCHOLOGICAL* ADVANTAGE OVER YOUR OPPONENTS

YOUR *FIRST DRIVE*, THEREFORE, BECOMES VITALLY IMPORTANT. HOW CAN YOU ENSURE THAT IT'S A GOOD ONE?

FIRSTLY, YOU MUST HAVE SEVERAL PRACTICE SWINGS TO HELP DISPEL ANY TENSION OR NERVOUSNESS

SECONDLY, IN YOUR PRACTICE SWINGS, CONCENTRATE ON GETTING *MAXIMUM CLUBHEAD SPEED* IN THE HITTING AREA

ACCELERATE

MANY DRIVES ARE MUFFED, ESPECIALLY ON THE FIRST TEE, BECAUSE THE PLAYER TRIES TO *STEER* HIS BALL INSTEAD OF HITTING CONFIDENTLY THROUGH IT

A match play tip

YOU ARE ACKNOWLEDGED TO BE THE WORLD'S GREATEST *MATCH PLAY* GOLFER, GARY. CAN YOU GIVE ME ANY TIPS?

OBVIOUSLY I CAN'T GIVE AWAY TOO MANY SECRETS UNTIL I RETIRE, TOM...

HOWEVER, ONE THING I ALWAYS DO IN *MATCH PLAY* IS TO *ATTACK* THE FIRST TWO HOLES. MANY GOLFERS PLAY *DEFENSIVELY* AT THE START OF A ROUND

I HAVE PROVED TIME AND TIME AGAIN THAT, IF I CAN WIN THE FIRST TWO HOLES, THIS PUTS MY OPPONENT UNDER *TREMENDOUS PRESSURE* WHICH HAS AN *ADVERSE EFFECT* ON THE MAN AND HIS GOLFSWING

Don't be demoralized

When to concede

Improve your thinking

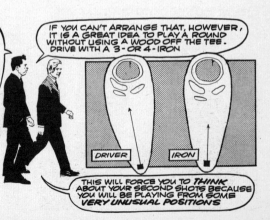

Study the green

In or out?

How to save nine shots

Good course management

section nine
Club Selection

Forget your pride

YOU HAVE *14 CLUBS*, TOM. ALWAYS USE THE ONE THAT WILL GET YOU UP TO THE GREEN *COMFORTABLY*. FORGET YOUR SILLY *PRIDE* THAT IS ALWAYS TELLING YOU TO TAKE A CLUB *LESS* THAN YOU REALLY NEED. YOU GET NO PRIZES FOR THAT!

SEE WHAT HAPPENS WHEN YOU *FORCE* A *3-IRON*, TOM? YOUR SWING IS *JERKY* AND *FLATTER* THAN USUAL

AND I'M IN THE TREES, GARY!

NOW, WITH A *4-WOOD*, YOU ARE ABLE TO SWING WITHIN YOURSELF, YOUR RHYTHM IS *SMOOTHER* AND YOUR *ARC* MORE UPRIGHT

A psychological benefit

GARY, THAT'S THE *BEST* SHOT I'VE HIT ALL DAY. WHAT WENT *RIGHT?*

FLASH BACK

IT'S VERY SIMPLE, IAIN. I MADE YOUR *CLUB SELECTION* FOR YOU AND YOU TRUSTED ME

WHEN YOU ADDRESSED THE BALL, YOU HAD NO NAGGING DOUBTS THAT YOU HAD TOO LITTLE OR TOO MUCH CLUB. THIS GAVE YOU THE *CONFIDENCE* TO SWING FREELY

THAT IS WHY I AM ALWAYS URGING YOU TO FIND OUT HOW FAR YOU HIT WITH *EACH* CLUB. THIS KNOWLEDGE IS OF TREMENDOUS *PSYCHOLOGICAL* BENEFIT TO A GOLFER

Never be short

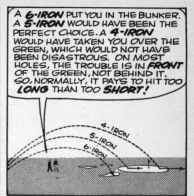

Don't be short

Swing easy and win

Judging distance

Relax and play well

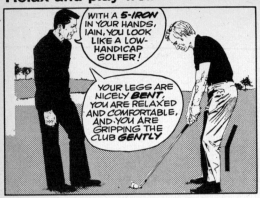

A more compact swing

4-wood or 2-iron

Stay alert

Think ahead

Think for yourself

Play within yourself

Be contented

103

section ten
From the Rough

Preventing a hook

WHENEVER I HAVE TO PLAY A SHORT WEDGE SHOT OUT OF *LONG GRASS*, I ALWAYS SEEM TO *HOOK* THE BALL, GARY!

TOM

THAT IS BECAUSE THE GRASS WRAPS ITSELF *AROUND* THE FACE OF THE CLUB AND *TWISTS* IT RIGHT OVER

WHEN PLAYING OUT OF LONG GRASS, I COUNTERACT THE TENDENCY TO HOOK BY HAVING THE FACE OF MY WEDGE SLIGHTLY *OPEN* AT ADDRESS

OPEN

THEN, I MAKE A *CONSCIOUS EFFORT* TO KEEP THE CLUB GOING *STRAIGHT THROUGH* TO THE TARGET, THUS PREVENTING MY WRISTS FROM *ROLLING OVER*

Mind that flower!

YOU WILL GET A "FLIER" HERE, IAIN, BECAUSE YOU ARE GOING TO HIT THAT *DANDELION* BEFORE YOU HIT THE BALL

WHEN THERE IS A FLOWER OR A WEED IN FRONT OF THE BALL, I DON'T *GROUND* MY CLUB AT ADDRESS

I AIM TO HIT THE *TOP* OF THE BALL, THUS AVOIDING THE FLOWER COMPLETELY. IT'S THE ONLY WAY TO KEEP CONTROL OF THE SHOT

Choose the right club

A rough tip

How to get out of a ditch

More club—less distance

Don't go too far

A time to "top"

Beware that perched up ball...

"Skull" the ball

section eleven
Trouble Shots

Limit your follow-through

Don't gamble

Cut your losses

Through the gap

A downslope hook

A difficult fade

The high shot

Beware low shots

A deliberate hook

Take more club

Playing off a hard surface

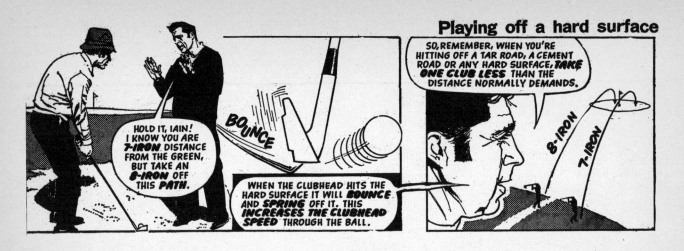

HOLD IT, IAIN! I KNOW YOU ARE 7-IRON DISTANCE FROM THE GREEN, BUT TAKE AN 8-IRON OFF THIS PATH.

WHEN THE CLUBHEAD HITS THE HARD SURFACE IT WILL BOUNCE AND SPRING OFF IT. THIS INCREASES THE CLUBHEAD SPEED THROUGH THE BALL.

SO, REMEMBER, WHEN YOU'RE HITTING OFF A TAR ROAD, A CEMENT ROAD OR ANY HARD SURFACE, TAKE ONE CLUB LESS THAN THE DISTANCE NORMALLY DEMANDS.

Take your punishment

IN GOLF, IAIN, YOU'VE GOT TO LEARN TO TAKE YOUR PUNISHMENT. IT'S CHEAPER IN THE END

DON'T, FOR EXAMPLE, TAKE A WOOD OUT OF A BUNKER IF THE BUNKER HAS A SIZABLE LIP

I'VE SEEN MANY PLAYERS DO THIS IN THE BRITISH OPEN AND LEAVE THE BALL IN THE SAND!

IF YOU GET INTO TROUBLE, ACCEPT THE FACT, TAKE THE CLUB THAT WILL GET YOU OUT. DON'T TRY THE IMPOSSIBLE

An easy way out

WOMEN ARE NOTORIOUSLY BAD BUNKER PLAYERS. THEY ARE TERRIFIED OF THE SHOT, AND THEY SIMPLY WILL NOT PRACTICE IT

BIG LIP

SMALL LIP

SOME BUNKERS, HOWEVER, HAVE VERY LITTLE "LIP", AND POOR SAND-PLAYERS OF BOTH SEXES SHOULD TAKE ADVANTAGE OF THIS BY USING A PUTTER

REMEMBER NOT TO GROUND THE CLUB WHEN ADDRESSING THE BALL

HIT THE BALL CLEANLY, FOLLOW RIGHT THROUGH, AND YOU OUGHT TO GET IT SOMEWHERE NEAR THE HOLE

The fairway trap

WHEN PLAYING FROM A FAIRWAY TRAP, IAIN, THE MINUTE YOU OPEN THE CLUBFACE YOU INCREASE THE RISK OF GETTING SAND BETWEEN CLUB AND BALL AT IMPACT

YOU SHOULD CLOSE THE CLUBFACE A BIT WHICH WILL PUT YOUR HANDS IN FRONT OF THE BALL AT ADDRESS. THIS WILL ENABLE YOU TO HIT THE BALL FIRST

CLOSED

HITTING THE SAND BEHIND THE BALL IS THE BIG DANGER IN A FAIRWAY TRAP!

section twelve
Equipment

Buying a glove

WHEN YOUR LEFT HAND *OPENS* AT THE TOP OF THE BACKSWING, TOM, YOU REALLY ARE IN TROUBLE. YOU WILL HAVE TO *RE-GRIP* ON THE DOWNSWING

TAKE YOUR GLOVE OFF AND SWING AGAIN

THAT'S BETTER. YOUR HANDS ARE STAYING CLOSED NOW

YOUR GLOVE WAS TOO *TIGHT*, TOM. WHEN YOU BUY A GLOVE MAKE SURE THAT YOU CAN SHUT YOUR HAND *COMFORTABLY* WITHOUT ANY FEELING OF *PRESSURE*

Check your grip

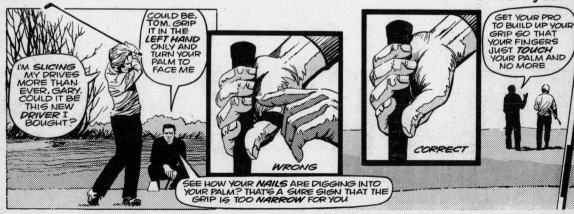

I'M *SLICING* MY DRIVES MORE THAN EVER, GARY. COULD IT BE THIS NEW *DRIVER* I BOUGHT?

COULD BE, TOM. GRIP IT IN THE *LEFT HAND* ONLY AND TURN YOUR PALM TO FACE ME

WRONG

CORRECT

GET YOUR PRO TO BUILD UP YOUR GRIP SO THAT YOUR FINGERS JUST *TOUCH* YOUR PALM AND NO MORE

SEE HOW YOUR *NAILS* ARE DIGGING INTO YOUR PALM? THAT'S A SURE SIGN THAT THE GRIP IS TOO *NARROW* FOR YOU

Thicken your grip

Support the club

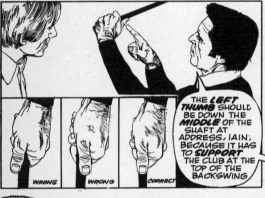

The secret of lighter clubs

Dead shafts

Lengthen your clubs

Suitable clubs

The wrong driver

The right clubs

The correct lie

Filing for height!

Have a re-groove

Don't slip!

section thirteen
Practice

Practising before a round

WHAT A WAY TO START A ROUND, GARY. I HIT A PERFECT DRIVE, A GOOD *4-IRON,* A TERRIBLE CHIP SHOT AND *THREE PUTTS!*

YOUR POOR *SHORT GAME* IS THE DIRECT RESULT OF THE WAY YOU *PRACTISED,* IAIN

YOU STARTED WITH A FEW *WEDGE* SHOTS AND GRADUALLY WORKED YOUR WAY UP TO YOUR *DRIVER* WHICH IS THE *CORRECT PROCEDURE*

YOU DIDN'T ALLOW FOR THE FACT, HOWEVER, THAT, WHEN YOU HIT SEVERAL TEE SHOTS IN SUCCESSION, YOU LOSE YOUR SENSE OF *TOUCH!*

I ALWAYS CONCLUDE MY PRACTICE SESSION BY HITTING A FEW *CHIP SHOTS* AND *PUTTS* SO THAT I REGAIN MY TOUCH BEFORE I STEP ONTO THAT FIRST TEE

Think of two things

WHAT ARE YOU WORKING ON, IAIN?

NOTHING IN PARTICULAR, GARY. I'M JUST HITTING A FEW BALLS BEFORE WE PLAY.

THAT IS A MISTAKE, IAIN. ALWAYS HAVE A DEFINITE OBJECTIVE WHEN YOU ARE PRACTISING.

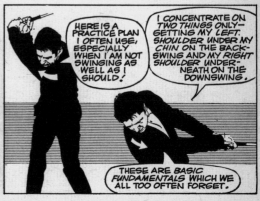

HERE IS A PRACTICE PLAN I OFTEN USE, ESPECIALLY WHEN I AM NOT SWINGING AS WELL AS I SHOULD!

I CONCENTRATE ON TWO THINGS ONLY— GETTING MY *LEFT* SHOULDER UNDER MY CHIN ON THE BACK-SWING AND MY *RIGHT* SHOULDER UNDER-NEATH ON THE DOWNSWING.

THESE ARE BASIC FUNDAMENTALS WHICH WE ALL TOO OFTEN FORGET.

Practice near trees

WHEN YOU HIT PRACTICE SHOTS TO A WIDE OPEN SPACE, IAIN, YOU ARE NOT REALLY *AIMING* AT ANYTHING IN PARTICULAR

CONSEQUENTLY, IT IS VERY HARD TO KNOW WHETHER YOU ARE HITTING THE BALL WELL OR NOT

ONE OF THE BEST THINGS YOU CAN DO IS TO HIT THROUGH *TREES*, PROVIDED THEY ARE NOT SO CLOSE THAT THERE IS ANY DANGER OF *RICOCHETS*

NOW YOU ARE FORCED TO *AIM CAREFULLY* EVERY TIME AND THIS ENCOURAGES YOU TO SWING BETTER

You can't see yourself

I HEAR YOU'VE BEEN PRACTISING HARD, IAIN !

YES, GARY! I'VE TRIED *TEN* DIFFERENT SWINGS SINCE I SAW YOU LAST, AND MY GAME IS *WORSE* THAN EVER !

THE REASON IS OBVIOUS, IAIN. YOUR WEIGHT IS MOVING ONTO YOUR *LEFT* FOOT ON THE BACKSWING WHICH MEANS THAT IT MUST FLOW ONTO YOUR *RIGHT* FOOT AS YOU HIT THROUGH. THIS IS BACK-TO-FRONT !

WRONG   CORRECT

UNFORTUNATELY WE CANNOT SEE *OURSELVES* SWING, IAIN. THAT IS WHY A VISIT TO THE *PRO* IS PREFERABLE TO SLOGGING AWAY ON YOUR OWN

Start at the bottom

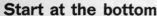

I SEE YOU'VE TAKEN MY ADVICE, IAIN, AND ARE WORKING ON GETTING A *SMOOTH FOLLOW-THROUGH*

BUT I'M NOT MAKING MUCH PROGRESS, GARY. THE BALL'S GOING ALL OVER THE PLACE

YOU'RE MAKING THE MISTAKE OF PRACTISING WITH YOUR DRIVER WHICH IS A DIFFICULT CLUB TO HANDLE WHEN YOU WANT TO GET THE *FEELING* OF SOME MOVEMENT IN GOLF YOU SHOULD ALWAYS START OFF WITH YOUR *WEDGE*

ONCE YOU HAVE MASTERED THE MOVEMENT WITH THE WEDGE, YOU CAN MOVE UP THROUGH THE CLUBS UNTIL, EVENTUALLY, YOU REACH THE DRIVER

Swing in stages

ONE WAY OF TRAINING YOURSELF TO KEEP YOUR HEAD STILL IS TO SWING IN STAGES, IAIN

FIRST HIT A LOT OF SHOTS WITH A WEDGE WHERE YOU ONLY SWING A *THIRD* BACK AND A *THIRD* THROUGH

THEN GO INTO YOUR *9-IRON* AND GO A LITTLE FURTHER BACK AND A LITTLE FURTHER THROUGH

THEN TAKE YOUR *6-IRON* AND GO *THREE-QUARTERS* BACK, *THREE-QUARTERS* THROUGH

FINALLY, GO ONTO YOUR DRIVER AND GO BACK *FULLY* AND THROUGH *FULLY*. THE BIG THING IS TO DO IT IN STAGES SO THAT YOU GET THE FEELING OF *KEEPING YOUR HEAD STILL*

Head and heels

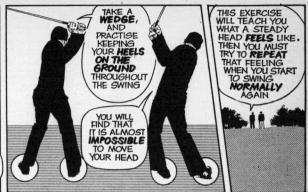

A three-to-one exercise

Not so fast

The one-arm swing

117

Swing a broom

Don't hit "heavy"

The way to success

Turn but don't sway

Play a tune

Purposeful practice

The practice swing

Practicing extension

Practice your backswing

Swinging in the plane

Competitive practice

Cutting the grass

YOUR FOLLOW-THROUGH IS FAR TOO *SHORT*, TOM. THAT PROVES THAT YOUR CLUB IS *SLOWING DOWN* BEFORE IT HITS THE BALL

WEEKEND GOLFERS TEND TO HIT *AT* THE BALL AS IF THERE WERE A *BRICK WALL* JUST IN FRONT OF THEM. YOU MUST HIT *RIGHT THROUGH* THE BALL

PRACTICE SWINGING IN *LONG GRASS* AND YOU WILL TRAIN YOURSELF TO *FOLLOW RIGHT THROUGH*

SCYTHE THE GRASS— DON'T USE A BALL

Encouraging a slow swing

SORRY I'M LATE, GARY. I'LL JUST HIT HALF A DOZEN *DRIVES*, THEN WE CAN GET STARTED

THAT WOULD BE A BIG MISTAKE, TOM. YOU'D BE FAR BETTER TO HIT A FEW *9-IRON* SHOTS

WITH THE *9-IRON*, YOU WILL BE FAR MORE LIKELY TO SWING *SLOWLY* AND *RHYTHMICALLY* WHICH IS WHAT YOU WANT TO DO OUT ON THE COURSE

THE DRIVER TENDS TO MAKE US SWING *FAST*, WHICH IS NOT DESIRABLE

On the practice green

I'M HOLING A FEW TODAY, GARY!

THAT'S NOT SURPRISING, TOM! YOU ARE PUTTING FROM THE *SAME SPOT* ALL THE TIME!

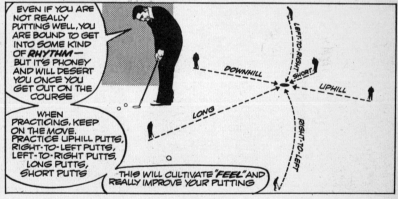

EVEN IF YOU ARE NOT REALLY PUTTING WELL, YOU ARE BOUND TO GET INTO SOME KIND OF *RHYTHM*— BUT IT'S PHONEY AND WILL DESERT YOU ONCE YOU GET OUT ON THE COURSE

WHEN PRACTICING, KEEP ON THE MOVE. PRACTICE UPHILL PUTTS, RIGHT-TO-LEFT PUTTS, LEFT-TO-RIGHT PUTTS, LONG PUTTS, SHORT PUTTS

THIS WILL CULTIVATE "FEEL" AND REALLY IMPROVE YOUR PUTTING

LEFT-TO-RIGHT

DOWNHILL

SHORT

UPHILL

LONG

RIGHT-TO-LEFT

Improve your shotmaking

ONCE A GOLFER IS HITTING THE BALL REASONABLY WELL, IAIN, HE SHOULD START TO EXPLORE THE *SUBTLETIES* OF *SHOTMAKING*

THE PLACE TO DO THIS IS ON THE *PRACTICE GROUND*

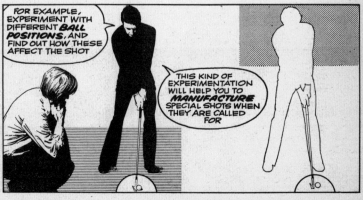

FOR EXAMPLE, EXPERIMENT WITH DIFFERENT *BALL POSITIONS*, AND FIND OUT HOW THESE AFFECT THE SHOT

THIS KIND OF EXPERIMENTATION WILL HELP YOU TO *MANUFACTURE* SPECIAL SHOTS WHEN THEY ARE CALLED FOR

section fourteen
Exercises

The need for fitness

ANY GOLFER WHO WANTS TO DO REALLY WELL MUST ENSURE THAT HE IS A *HUNDRED PER CENT FIT*

THIS IS WHY I KEEP ON RECOMMENDING PHYSICAL EXERCISES SUCH AS *SKIPPING, PRESS-UPS, RUNNING*

THE *STRONGER* YOU ARE, THE *FURTHER* YOU WILL HIT YOUR DRIVES—AND THIS IS IMPORTANT FOR THREE *REASONS* . . .

IF YOU OUTDRIVE YOUR OPPONENT YOU CAN WALK MORE *SLOWLY* TO YOUR SECOND SHOT AS HE WILL HAVE TO HIT FIRST. SLOW WALKING ENCOURAGES A *SLOW-TEMPO* SWING

SECONDLY, YOU WILL HAVE *LONGER* TO THINK ABOUT YOUR NEXT SHOT

THIRDLY, YOU WILL BE ABLE TO USE A *SHORTER* IRON THAN YOUR OPPONENT, WHICH IS AN ADVANTAGE

A paper exercise

ON THE WHOLE, WEEKEND GOLFERS NEED TO STRENGTHEN THEIR *HANDS, WRISTS* AND *FOREARMS*

HERE IS AN EXERCISE THAT WILL DO JUST THAT. TAKE TWO PAGES OF A NEWSPAPER AND CRUMPLE THEM INTO A BALL USING ONLY THE FINGERS OF ONE HAND

DON'T STOP UNTIL THE NEWSPAPER IS IN A *TIGHT BALL,* BY WHICH TIME YOUR HAND SHOULD BE *ACHING.* THEN REPEAT THE EXERCISE USING YOUR OTHER HAND

IF YOU DO THIS ONCE A DAY FOR 3 MONTHS, I GUARANTEE YOU WILL HIT THE BALL *15 YARDS FURTHER*

Increase your strength

YOUR ARMS ARE *BENDING* AT IMPACT, TOM, AND YOUR BODYWEIGHT IS *LAGGING BEHIND*

YOUR WEIGHT MUST BE THRUST *FORWARD* AND YOUR ARMS *EXTENDED* TO GET ALL YOUR *POWER* INTO THE SHOT

OBVIOUSLY, *STRENGTH* IS VERY IMPORTANT, AND I FIND THAT THIS *ISOMETRIC* EXERCISE BUILDS UP MY ARMS. WITH YOUR LEFT HAND AGAINST A TREE OR A WALL, PUSH HARD ACROSS TO THE LEFT WITH YOUR WHOLE BODY, KEEPING YOUR HEAD STILL. HOLD THIS FOR *SIX SECONDS*, THEN RELAX

Keeping fit

I OFTEN SEE YOU HAVE A FEW SWINGS *LEFT-HANDED*, GARY. WHY DO YOU DO THIS?

IT'S ONE OF MY DAILY EXERCISES TO PREVENT *SLIPPED DISCS* AND *BACKACHE*, TOM. MY SPINE IS BENT IN THE OPPOSITE DIRECTION TO WHEN I AM SWINGING *RIGHT-HANDED*

FOR THE SAME REASON I LIKE TO ROTATE MY HIPS *CLOCKWISE* BECAUSE THEY NORMALLY HAVE TO WORK FAST IN AN *ANTI-CLOCKWISE* DIRECTION

THESE EXERCISES ARE *ESPECIALLY IMPORTANT* FOR PEOPLE WHO PLAY A *LOT* OF GOLF. THEY HELP TO *COUNTERACT* THE STRESSES WHICH THE GAME PUTS ON THE SPINE

THE THIRD THING I DO EVERY DAY IS TO TOUCH MY TOES THEN ARCH MY BACK

Strengthen your left hand

YOUR RIGHT HAND IS MUCH STRONGER THAN YOUR LEFT, TOM. THIS IS WHY YOUR FOLLOW-THROUGH IS *CRAMPED*

FOR A RIGHT-HANDED GOLFER, IT IS A DISTINCT ADVANTAGE IF THE *LEFT HAND* IS THE STRONGER ONE. THIS WAS ONE OF BEN HOGAN'S ASSETS

YOU CAN INCREASE THE STRENGTH OF YOUR LEFT HAND BY *SQUEEZING A RUBBER BALL*

IT IS THE LEFT HAND WHICH *GUIDES* THE CLUB THROUGH THE BALL, THEREFORE IT MAKES SENSE TO ENSURE THAT IT WILL NOT BE OVERPOWERED BY THE RIGHT. A *STRONG LEFT HAND* KEEPS THE CLUB *ON LINE* AND LEADS TO GOOD *EXTENSION* THROUGH THE BALL

Play well all the time

WHY DO I ALWAYS PLAY THE *FIRST* NINE HOLES REASONABLY WELL, GARY, AND THEN GO TO PIECES?

BECAUSE YOUR LEGS LET YOU DOWN, TOM. AS THEY GET TIRED, THEY BECOME *STRAIGHT* AT ADDRESS AND YOUR WHOLE SWING IS AFFECTED

YOU CAN HAVE THE BEST SWING IN THE WORLD, BUT IF YOU DON'T DEVELOP *GOOD LEG MUSCLES* THROUGH EXERCISES SUCH AS SKIPPING, RUNNING IN PLACE, CYCLING, YOU WILL NEVER ACHIEVE YOUR *FULL POTENTIAL*

GOOD

BAD

Stretch your muscles

A wide swing arc

Strengthen your left hand

Be a body-swinger!

section fifteen
Common Faults & Cures

Check your alignment

Check your aim

Lining up the feet

Beat that tension

Think right—start right

The "weekender's crouch"

Square up

A dangerous practice swing

A good beginning

The head test

Tuck in your elbow

Swing within yourself

Controlling the clubhead

YOUR CLUBHEAD IS POINTING TO THE *LEFT* OF THE TARGET, TOM. THIS IS CALLED *LAYING THE CLUB OFF*

WHEN YOU DO THIS YOU CAN HOOK, SLICE OR HIT ANY KIND OF BAD SHOT

I KNOW THE CLUB SHOULD POINT TO THE TARGET AT THE TOP OF THE SWING, GARY, BUT WHAT CAN I DO TO ACHIEVE THIS?

TO TARGET

FORGET THE CLUBHEAD, TOM, AND CONCENTRATE ON YOUR LEFT *THUMB*. MAKE SURE THAT IT POINTS THE WAY YOU WANT TO GO. IT IS EASIER TO GET YOUR THUMB TO DO WHAT YOU WANT THAN THE CLUBHEAD

A false pivot

WHEN YOU ALLOW YOUR LEFT ARM TO *BEND*, IAIN, YOU GET WHAT I CALL A *FALSE* PIVOT

KEEP YOUR ARM *STRAIGHT*, AND YOU WILL FEEL THE STORED-UP ENERGY

IT IS BETTER TO HAVE A SLIGHTLY SHORTER BACKSWING AND A STRAIGHT LEFT ARM THAN A LONG BACKSWING AND A BENT ARM

A monthly check

IAIN, I'D LIKE YOU TO TELL ME IF MY HEAD *RISES* WHEN I TAKE THE CLUB BACK

IF ANYTHING, IT *DROPS* A FRACTION OF AN INCH, GARY!

GOOD! I DON'T MIND THAT!

THIS IS SOMETHING EVERY GOLFER SHOULD HAVE CHECKED *MONTHLY*, OR WHENEVER HE IS PLAYING POORLY. WHEN YOUR HEAD STARTS RISING UP ON THE BACKSWING, IT'S SURPRISING HOW QUICKLY YOUR GAME CAN SIMPLY *FALL APART!*

Reduce the backswing

PEOPLE WHO ARE DESK-BOUND ALL WEEK, AND ELDERLY GOLFERS, OFTEN FIND IT DIFFICULT TO HAVE A *FULL BACKSWING* WITHOUT BENDING THE LEFT ARM!

WHEN THE SHOULDERS TURN PAST A CERTAIN POINT, THE LEFT ARM SIMPLY *COLLAPSES*.

IN THESE CASES, IT IS ADVISABLE TO REDUCE THE BACKSWING SO THAT THE LEFT ARM CAN REMAIN *STRAIGHT*.

ALTHOUGH THIS REDUCES THE ARC OF THE SWING, THAT IS NOT TOO BIG A PRICE TO PAY BECAUSE, WITH A BENT LEFT ARM, THERE IS A TENDENCY TO *QUIT ON THE SHOT*—AND THAT IS A TERRIBLE FAULT!

Three checks

Increase your backswing

Don't collapse

Time to pause

Weight transference

Proper weight transference

Proper weight transference

Mind that heel

Heel and head

Shifting the weight

A little slide

Don't turn too far

The rope trick

Keep your heel down

How to stay on line

A little first aid

Speed is essential

Rhythm centre

Keeping your rhythm

Regaining rhythm

Don't hurry

Swing flatter

Swing fully every time

Swing wide

Stop swaying

Turn—don't slide

Exaggerate!

Stay over the ball

Retain your power

Maintain the angle

Don't hit too early

Snapping the elbow

Lead with the hip

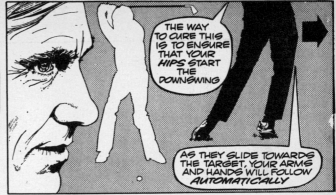

The need for good foot work

Hit the ball first

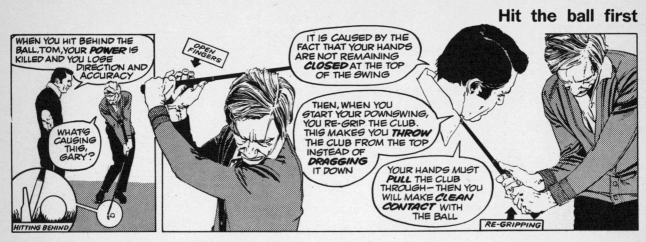

Hitting heavy

Watch that ball

Head up

Constant reminders

The head cure

Don't watch the ball

Stay in focus

Hitting from the top

Pulldown

Raise your wrist

Speedy hands

The power triangle

The golden rule

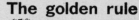

Don't straighten too soon

Extend for distance

Stretch your imagination

Hands not ball

Right through the ball

Shoulder to chin

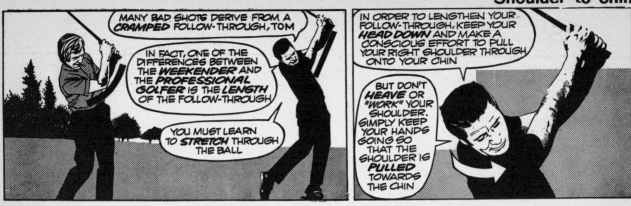

Extend for distance

Underneath the head

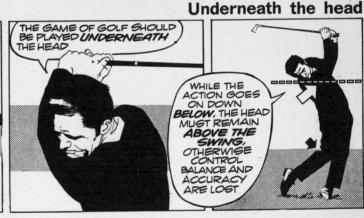

The tension points

The corkscrew heel

Be a bow

Don't fall back

Punch your weight

The shoulder check

Improvement at last

Stopping the long irons

Bisect your head

Open your stance

Stop hooking your putts

Release—don't shank

Accuracy with the short irons

Hooks and slices

"Backhanding" the ball

Don't break too quickly

Hooking into trouble

Hooking into the wind

Don't chop and change

Swing the grip

Curing a hook

How to stop slicing

Why you slice

The spinning heel

A natural turn

Squeeze the club

Stop slicing

Time to cure a slice

section sixteen
Bad Weather

Gauging the wind

I ALLOWED FOR THE WIND, GARY, YET I'VE MISSED THE GREEN BY A *MILE!*

YOU MADE A *FUNDAMENTAL MISTAKE*, IAIN!

YOU JUDGED THE WIND BY LOOKING AT THE *FLAG*. THAT IS A VERY BAD THING TO DO BECAUSE OFTEN LITTLE, SWIRLING CURRENTS OF AIR CAN GIVE YOU A *WRONG IMPRESSION*

ALWAYS LOOK AT THE *TOPS OF THE TREES* TO SEE WHAT WAY THE WIND IS BLOWING. WITH YOUR *SHORT IRONS* YOUR BALL IS GOING TO GO *ABOVE* THE TREES, SO IT MAKES SENSE TO SEE WHAT THE WIND IS DOING UP THERE

Swinging in the wind

YOUR SWING IS FAR TOO *UPRIGHT* FOR THESE WINDY CONDITIONS, TOM

A FLATTER SWING IS MUCH BETTER BECAUSE IT KEEPS THE BALL *LOWER*

SO *SHORTEN* YOUR SWING IN WIND, AND KEEP IT *COMPACT*

ARNOLD PALMER AND *BEN HOGAN* SWING ON THE FLATTISH SIDE. THEY BOTH KNOW HOW TO HANDLE THE WIND

JACK NICKLAUS AND *JOHNNY MILLER*, WITH THEIR VERY UPRIGHT SWINGS, HIT THE BALL VERY HIGH. I WOULD NOT CALL THEM GOOD WIND PLAYERS

Driving in the wind

Play into the wind

Limit your swing

(panel 1) IT IS A BAD THING TO *OVERSWING*, TOM—PARTICULARLY IN *WINDY* CONDITIONS

(panel 2) A LONG SWING IS MORE DIFFICULT TO CONTROL. THERE IS MORE TIME FOR THINGS TO GO WRONG—MORE TIME TO BE BLOWN OFF BALANCE

(panel 3) SO *LIMIT* YOUR BACKSWING—MAKE IT MORE *COMPACT*. THEN YOU WILL HAVE A BETTER CHANCE OF PLAYING WELL IN WIND

Square, closed and open

IN NORMAL CONDITIONS, THE CLUBFACE SHOULD BE *SQUARE* AT ADDRESS

SQUARE

IN A LEFT-TO-RIGHT WIND IT SHOULD BE *CLOSED*

CLOSED

WHEN THE WIND IS BLOWING RIGHT-TO-LEFT, THE CLUBFACE SHOULD BE *OPEN*

BY OPENING OR CLOSING THE CLUBFACE AT ADDRESS, YOU WILL IMPART SIDESPIN TO THE BALL WHICH WILL HELP IT FIGHT THE WIND

OPEN

You mustn't hook

IN A *RIGHT-TO-LEFT* WIND, TOM, THE LAST THING YOU WANT IS TO *HOOK* THE BALL

BUT I'VE DONE IT!

YOU MUST TRY TO GET THE CLUBFACE TO STAY *FACING THE HOLE LONGER* IN ORDER TO HOLD THE BALL INTO A RIGHT-TO-LEFT WIND

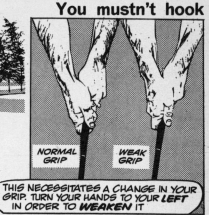

NORMAL GRIP

WEAK GRIP

THIS NECESSITATES A CHANGE IN YOUR GRIP. TURN YOUR HANDS TO YOUR *LEFT* IN ORDER TO *WEAKEN* IT

Hit higher

I THOUGHT I WOULD EASILY REACH THE GREEN, GARY, BUT I'VE LANDED *SHORT*

YOU DIDN'T ALLOW FOR THE *WIND*, TOM

WHEN THE WIND IS BEHIND YOU, IT *BEATS* THE BALL DOWN

THEREFORE, YOU SHOULD TRY TO HIT A LITTLE BIT *HIGHER* THAN NORMAL WHEN THE WIND IS AT YOUR BACK

WIND BEHIND

NORMAL DAY

Playing the wind

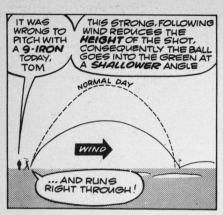

Putting the brakes on

A 4-point plan

An imaginary green

Open the clubface

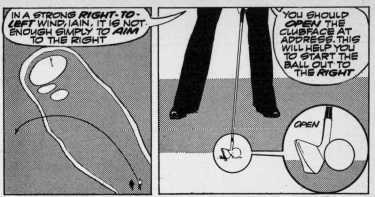

Chip into the wind

A wide putting stance

Don't address the ball!

Beating the wind

Don't ignore the wind

Playing in cold weather

Don't re-grip

Beware the umbrella

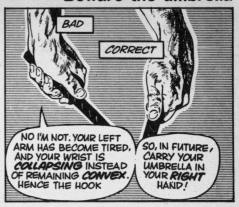

Wet weather driving

Slow down in the rain

Change of address

Highlights of Gary Player's Tournament Record

1956
Winner—Dunlop Tournament, England
Winner—South African Open
Winner—Ampol Tournament, Yara Yara, Melbourne, Australia
Winner—Egyptian Medal Play

1957
Winner—Australian PGA

1958
Winner—Australian Open
Winner—Kentucky Derby Open

1959
Winner—South African PGA
Winner—Victoria Open
*Winner—British Open

1960
Winner—South African Open
Winner—South African PGA

1961
*Winner—Masters
Winner—Lucky International Open
Winner—Sunshine Open

1962
*Winner—U.S. PGA
Winner—Australian Open
Winner—Transvaal Open

1963
Winner—San Diego Open
Winner—Australian Open
Winner—Sponsored 5,000

1964
Winner—Pensacola Open
Winner—"500" Festival Open
Winner—South African Masters

1965
*Winner—U.S. Open
Winner—South African Open
Winner—Canadian Cup Singles

Winner—Australian Open
Winner—Piccadilly Match Play
Winner—NTL Challenge Cup
Winner—World Series of Golf
Winner—World Cup, Individual

1966
Winner—Piccadilly Match Play
Winner—South African Open
Winner—Natal Open
Winner—Transvaal Open

1967
Winner—Dunlop Masters, South Africa
Winner—South African Open

1968
Winner—British Open
Winner—World Series of Golf
Winner—Piccadilly World Match Play
Winner—South African Open
Winner—Natal Open
Winner—Western Province Open
Winner—Australian Wills Masters

1969
Winner—Tournament of Champions
Winner—South African Open
Winner—South African PGA
Winner—Australian Open

1970
Winner—Greater Greensboro Open
Winner—Australian Open
Winner—Dunlop International

1971
Winner—Greater Jacksonville Open
Winner—National Airlines Open
Winner—Piccadilly Match Play Championship
Winner—Dunlop Masters, South Africa
Winner—General Motors Open
Winner—Western Province Open

1972
Winner—Greater New Orleans Open
Winner—Brazilian Open

Winner—U.S. PGA
Winner—South African Open
Winner—World Series of Golf

1973
Winner—Southern Open
Winner—Piccadilly Match Play

1974
Winner—Masters
Winner—Danny Thomas, Memphis
Winner—British Open
Winner—Brazilian Open
Winner—Australian Open

1975
Winner—Lancome Trophy
Winner—South African Open
Winner—General Motors International Classic

1976
Winner—Dunlop Masters, South Africa
Winner—South African Open

1977
Winner—World Cup, Individual
Winner—South African Open

1978
Winner—Masters
Winner—Tournament of Champions
Winner—Houston Open

1979
Winner—South African PGA
Winner—South African Open
Winner—Sun City Classic (South Africa)

1980
Winner—Chile Open
Winner—Houphouet-Biogny Trophy (Ivory Coast)

The Grand Slam of Golf